THE LAST NIGHT

ANSHARAH NOAH

Made with ♥ on the Notion Press Platform
www.notionpress.com

Contents

CAST

Kabir

He was not a male model , but he should have been .

He had a dashing personality and a cosmic smile .

He was blessed with dark coal black eyes and with 6.2 ft height .

He always wore ritzy clothes and his expensive aroma was appealing.

He had defined cheeckbones and bristy eyebrows.

His face was half covered by his classic -trimmed full beard .

His personality was good , but Love Life wasn't .

"Hello Reader"

"

I am Kabir .
I am being forced to marry by family .
"

"Tomorrow is my wedding,
I invite you to celebrate my wedding or my heart's funeral .
I am still in Love with my ex -girlfriend "Sarah".
She Left me without any reason ."

Taanish

He was, well, different from all others.
He was handsome, not perhaps in the conventional sense,
but he had that appearance which could make him stand out in the
crowd.

He was fair, almost pale white.
His coal dark eyes were as deep and expressive,
where you could get lost if you stared long enough.

"Hello Reader"

"

My name is Taanish , a confidant person .
Friend of Kabir ,Arjun and Muraad . "

"

I am good at keeping secrets ,
You can share your secrets with me. I won't tell anyone .
Infact , I am in Love with someone i won't reveal the name
"
.

Muraad

"He was a compact, clearcut man,
with precise features, a lot of very soft black hair,
and thoughtful dark brown eyes.
He had a look of wariness, which could change
when he felt relaxed or happy."

"Hello Reader"

"

I am Muraad .
Friend of Kabir , Arjun and Taanish . "

"

I am serious kind of person .I Love to be the way I am ,
it doesn't matter what people think of me or call me . "

Arjun

"Arjun was a tall man with powerful shoulders, a fierce dark
face,
and eyes that seemed to flash and glitter with savage laughter.
He had the flat brown eyes and strong facial features .
He was intelligent and humorous , funny and entertaining ."

"Hello Reader "

"

I am Arjun .
Friend of Kabir , Taanish and Muraad.
I consider myself an outgoing , fun-loving person .
I just Love to travel the world .
Infact next week I am planning to go Bali ,
Will you join me "

"THOU - YOU"

"THY- YOUR"

Chapter1

THE LAST NIGHT

A Night Before Wedding

TIME 8:00 PM

(KABIR AND ARJUN TALKING)

" Kabir are thou exicted?
tomorrow is thy wedding night ,
Asked Arjun ,
While wiring the bulb light .

Oh brother Arjun ,
This is marriage arranged,
There will be no exictement
Am i right ?

I still love her (Sarah),
but She is gone ,
made my life Black ,
I trusted her
but she stabbed in the back .

No , kabir don't be sad ,
there was a Love gap.

(Kabir Laughed and said)

Oh Brother Arjun,

What love ? She cheated and loyalty lacked.

Arjun said ,

Oh brother don't be sad ,

Have some snacks .

GOSSIPING

Time 09:00 PM

"Raat bhar jhoomenge ,

Aasmaan ghoomenge,

Chand ye choomenge ,

Taaron kemaarenge phere ,

Ude dil Befikre ,Ude dil befikre "

Singing dancing Taanish stepped inside ,

Hugged kabir ,and said " lets go for long drive ,

Kabir denied ," I am not able to move ,

Thou (Taanish) say , What about thy life .

Arjun said ,

"Tomorrow is the big day our life ,

Thou (Taanish) will fly to bangkok,

And thou (Kabir) wedding night .

Together this is our Last night .

Arjun asked Taanish ,

How is thy to be wife ,

Show some pics ,

No mode hide.

Kabir Laughed and said ,"tell her name ,

Or else I could also bribe .

Taanish replied ,

"Naam liya to badnaam hojyegi ,

Parde mein rakhaa hai usse ,

Woh sare aam hojayegi ..

(All Laughed)

Chapter2

BETRAYAL

1. *MELANCHOLY KABIR*
2. *GIVE THE NAME*
3. *A FRIEND'S BETRAYAL*

Melancholy Kabir

TIME 10:00PM

Kabir singing

" Raanjhe Ishq Vich Hoye Qurbaan, Kinne Mirze Bhi De Gaye
Jaan,
Yeh Khel Bada Badnaam Re, Jhuthe Khwaab Dekhawe,
Toote Kanch Ke Tukdo Pe, Mua Ishq Nachaawe...
Seene Saari Raat Dard Jagaave,
Ik Pal Chain Na Aave,... -"

Arjun said

Oh Murad thanks God came here ,

This melancholy Kabir ,
I cannot more bear ,
Murad why so late here ,

Oh Murad dear ,
Come and sit near .

Song playing in the background .

Arjun asked Taanish

Taanish let's go Out ,
before night gets dark , and brightness Lack,
To buy more drink and some more Snacks,
Kabir and Murad thou guys continue ,
We will be back .

(Taanish and Arjun exited through the door)

Give the Name

Kabir ,I want talk thou urgent before sun bright ,
Said Murad while having a bite ,

Kabir asked ,
What happened Murad ,
thou are not looking alright .

Murad replied

"Oh Melancholy Kabir
It's about (Sarah) thy Ex to be bride ,
I remember the night when she left
and thou Cried .

She ghosted thou and
dissappeared from thy sight .

Kabir i found that guy ,
with whom thou Ex flied.

In the world of no shadow ,
She Cheated and thy heart died.

Kabir growled

"Murad tell me the name
Of the guy , who played good games

Give me the name Murad ,
Tell me the name
of the guy, who snatched my Love ,
without any shame .

A Friend's Betrayal

TIME 11:00PM

Muraad said ,
"He made us fool ,
Indeed we are foolish ,

I saw him and sarah together ,
He is none other than our friend **Taanish .**

Tomorrow they both will fly to bangkok ,
i saw their tickets
When his phone was unlock ,
Bro Kabir , Do something ,
It's already 11 ' O Clock .

(Kabir shattered a wine glass in his hand out of anger)

Oh Muraad,
I was sad ,
but now I am mad ,
I thought Taanish is my buddy ,
but he betrayed ,Indeed he is bad .

Muraad consoled kabir

oh melancholy kabir , don't be sad ,
Now you know the truth just be Glad,

Tell Bastard Taanish that ,
In playing games ,
You are his Dad .

Chapter3

UNPLANNED PLAN

1. PLANNED MURDER

PLANNED MURDER

TIME 11:30 PM

Kabir continued

" It would be my last wish ,
To punish the devil Taanish ,

I will prepare a meal .
It would be his last dish ,

From the Ocean of Love ,
He took my fish ,
Indeed he is rascal ,
And ,
Sarah is a Bitch .

Murad asked ,

Night is getting Darker ,
Kabir are you planning a murder ?

Thou are not a gangster ,
Let the God punish him

Don't wet your hand in the blood of Gutter .

"No murad ,
let me color my hand with my friend's blood .
thou don't know , how much i cried for that Slut,
If i collected my tears,
Then it would be a Ocean Or flood ."

Murad said ,

"Okay Kabir , What's the plan ?
Sealed your feelings
Love , Emotions, Sympathy ,
Now everything is ban .
Now we will punish that bastard ,
Yes we will and We can .

Poison in a bun
or you will shot him by your gun .

Kabir replied

"neither poison in bread or bun ,
nor i will shoot him by my gun ."

Then how kabir ?

" With dagger ".

A dagger ?

Yes.

Chapter 4

SARAH

SARAH

Kabir thinking about his Ex girlfriend Sarah

"Oh My beautiful Sarah ,"

"

I still remember the day when I saw you for the first time,
you were wearing Black top and blue jeans."

"I was fascinated by your brown eyes ,
and by your bra size."

"

By your pink glossy lips,
and by your nice hips."

"

By Your Long black hair ,
and by your complexion fair."

"

By Your curvy figure

and by your thick lip filler. "

"*By your thick thighs
and by your charming eyes* "

"*5.5ft is your height ,
You fascinated me by wearing clothes tight.* "

PART 1

"Oh My beloved Sarah,"

"You keep secret in your eyes
many secret and malicious lies
secret lies in your brown eyes ."

"I still remember the feeling i felt when we first kissed ,
I wanted to do more , but condoms were missed."

"I still remember the day when you call me mine .
my heart smile and eyes shine ."

"Oh My Dear Sarah ,
I remember the night ,
When we make Love all night .
Candlelight dinner and our pillow-Fight ."

"Oh My Darling Sarah ,
I still remember the night,"

"

We had sex on the floor ,
When 47 was our sex- score ."

"

Then you left and closed the door.
*It was the dawn ,and the time was only four.**"*

PART 2

"I still remember the day when you said
" Kabir, It's not working anymore ".
and you left and closed the door .
still i tried but
but you ghosted me and ignore . "

"

Why sarah why ?
Why did you cheat on me ? "

"

Why did you leave me ?
Why did you ghost me ? "

"All you did for Taanish ?
My friend Taanish ?
Seriously Taanish? "

"Has he ordered your favourite wine ?
At Your favourite restaurant or home-dine? "

"

Has he licked your vagina and spine ?

Has he made you smile and eyes shine . "

"*May be his dick is longer than mine ,*
May be he is making you happy and fine. "

"*Oh my dear Sarah ,*
I thought you are mine ,
But this time , you have crossed the line . "

"*Oh My sweetheart Sarah ,*
I thought your heart is big as your breast .
But you are the Nightmare with sheild of musing
dressed. "

"*Oh Sarah ,* "

"

I wanted to make you my wife ,
for the rest of the life .
But you cheated on me .
I will kill that bastard with my dagger or knife . "

Chapter5

BLOODSHED

1. *MURDER*
2. *FRIEND TO FOE*

MURDER

TIME 12:00AM

"Hey kabir ,
what happened , ?
you are only physically here ." said Murad .

(Taanish entered in the room)

Taanish said

" Hey guys , i bought some food ,
Kabir dear , Why you look so rude ,
Arjun is parking the car,
I am here to change your mood . "

Kabir growled and asked Taanish

"Tell me Taanish , who is your girlfriend ?
tell me the name "

" benaam mohabbat ko badnaam hojaane do
Us bewafaa ko sare-aam ho jaane do ,
Bahot achhi nibhaayi hai dosti tumne
Ab is dosti mein khud ko Qurbaan hojaane do."

Kabir what happened , you are not looking alright . said Taanish .

Kabir started singing and dancing around Taanish .

"Dost - dost naa rahaa ,

Pyaar -pyaar na rahaa ,

Saare -bhed khul gaye koi raazdaar naa rahaaa,

Ab kisi ka mere dil mein intezaar na rahaa ,

Zindagi hume tera aitbaar na rahaa ,

Aitbaar na rahaa ."

Taanish asked Murad

" Murad , what happened , why kabir is acting so weird ? "

Murad replied " I am sorry "

Sorry for what ?

Kabir stabbed Taanish with a dagger .

TANISH DIED

FRIEND TO FOE

TIME 01:00 AM

(Arjun entered in the room)

He saw the deadbody of Taanish
he cried and said

"So thou have fullfilled thy lust ,
thy hand is full of blood
Nor sky nor earth ,
From dawn to dusk ,
No one will hide thy evil musk ."

night hides the secret ,
day reveal ,
thou killed thy own friend
Don't you feel .

Kabir said
"Don't tell anyone and ,
keep your lips sealed."

Arjun replied
" My lips will not be seal ,
I will tell everyone ,

And your skin will be peel ."

(Arjun attaked Kabir to take revenge of Taanish accidently)

Arjun killed by kabir

Arjun died .

Chapter 6

GUILT

1. REGRET

REGRET

TIME 02:00 AM

Kabir said to Murad

"

"Oh brother Murad ,
I have colored my hand with blood ,
i was innocent ,but now in sin of flood .
What shall i do now ,
This night is evil and crud .""

"" Bro , I cannot survive in this land ,
i will not marry , Wed is banned
Will all the water in the ocean ,
Can Wash this blood from my hand ?""

"NO"

"NO"

"NO"

"No the color of Ocean will turn into Red ,
Now my brothers are dead ,"

"

In the wicked world ,
I will never Love or Wed. "

"*"Oh , Murad you go and fly ,*
Fly to Dubai and job apply .
Thou will get the job ,
Thou are much Qualified. "

No kabir ,

Don't fear ,

Let me clear

I cannot leave you alone here ,

keep my words in your ear .

Lets hide the deadbodies

far from here .

Kabir replied

" Murad you just go from here .

and don't come near .

This Sin is mine ,

And i cannot be fine .

Let me surrender myself to cops ,

Or let me die here
Having list of emotions
but Guilt is on the Top .

Muraad just go from here ,
Go anywhere ,
Just not here ,

Murad exits .

Chapter 7

SARAH AGAIN

1. A MESSAGE

A MESSAGE

Time 03:00 AM

Kabir's phone rang ,
A message from Sarah

"" Hi Kabir
It's Your beloved Sarah , "

"Today is the Last night ,
Thy last virgin night "

"

I am far away from your sight ,
May God fill thy life with bright light ,
Only brightness ,no more dark Night . "

"My Love for thou is pure ,
I am suffering from disease which ,
Can not be cure ,
I will not survive more ,
Yes I am sure . "

"I did not wanted to hurt thou with truth ,
I never cheated thou ,
Left thou with ruth , "

" "

" *Our mutual friend Taanish knows this well ,*
Living without thou is living in hell . "

" *Am suffering from non -curable disease*
All Day and All Night , Dawn or Dusk ,
I am coughing and sneeze . "

" *Tomorrow*
Me , Taanish and my family
Leaving for Bangkok ,
Around 9 'o Clock . "

" *For the treatment of disease*
And I know it cannot be cure ,
But May be I can
survive 6 month More . "

.

" *Taanish and his boyfriend helped me a lot ,*
Yes he is Gay , and he is tying a knot. "

"

That's the reason he never revealed his Lover name .
Cuz he thought ,being Gay is such a Shame . "

"*Now I am telling you the truth Cuz Today ,*
is thy Last Night before wedding . "

"

I pray to God ,
To fill thy Life with bright light .
Time heals ,
And Everything will be alright . "